Teach Your Child

Homophones Vocabulary Builder 1

Mobile Learning Help for Active Parents

(Teach Your Child and Yourself Homophones)

Dova Lael

www.DovaSpellingCity.com

PARENTS

Do you know that children with the best vocabularies get the best grades in school and can go on to be the most successful in their chosen careers?

Are you aware that:

- Better vocabulary = better income?
- The more words a child knows, the greater that child's success?
- Just learning 10 words can expose your son or daughter to 90 more?

What does this mean?

Your child's ability to use his given language is the key to all his learning.

You as a caring parent must ensure that your son or daughter has a good vocabulary. **The "Teach Your Child and Yourself" series is designed to help you do just that.**

With the help of this workbook, your ward can learn 10 words a day using 3 easy steps. There are 5 lists for a minimum of 50 words. And since learning 10 words can expose your ward to 90 more, that's **a potential vocabulary boost for your child of 5 x (10 + 90) = 500 words!**

What are Homophones

Two words are homophones if they sound the same, but have different spellings and different meanings (e.g. stake and steak).

Why are homophones important?

Did you notice these words on the book cover? **Eye eight stake** (I ate steak).

Your heir would never master the English language or succeed at school making mistakes like these in his writing. At any rate he (or she) would have a pretty difficult time trying to eat a stake!

Is a homophone a homonym?

Homophones should not be confused with *homonyms* which are words that have the same spelling and pronunciation but different meanings depending on how they are used. (e.g. *cricket* - an insect and *cricket* - a game)

You will easily recognize the many homonyms in this book.

How to use This Book

First determine if you need this book. **Scan the QR code below** or go to **www.dovaspellingcity.com/hpre1** and have your ward take Pretest 1.

How this book is organized

There are 5 lists for a minimum of 50 words.

Each word is listed with its homophone or homophones and its meaning or use.

Each list is followed by 5 activities to help your "pupil" master the words in the list. These include puzzles, games and quizzes. Answers are at the back of the book.

Next there is a list of all the words taught in this book followed by 2 review exercises covering all the words presented in the 5 lists.

The final exercise is the Test Yourself quiz that checks whether your protégé understands the use of the homophones in this book.

There is also a bonus chapter from the next volume in this series.

The System:

Review, Practise, Test.

The Steps:

- Read through the list at the beginning of the chapter
- Use activities 1, 2 and 3 to practise
- Test yourself using the Spelling Challenge quiz (Activity 4)

Activity 5 can be used for additional practice or for revision at a later date.

Do this for all 5 lists.

A System Within a System

If you followed the system above, your ward would have reviewed and practised at least 50 words. Now he should test himself on those 50 words using the Review Exercises and the Test Yourself quiz.

An Additional Mobile Friendly Resource for the Active Parent

Adventures in Homophones is ideal for the active parent and child. It is an online game that you can also download to your iPad for use on the move.

After download it can be used **without** an internet connection.

Get it here: www.dovaspellingcity.com/aih1 or **scan the QR code on the next page.**

Finally... Teach Yourself

You too can benefit from using this workbook. You can use it before your child uses it (or with your child) to learn the words or as a refresher. **You too can improve your vocabulary and create success for yourself.**

Adventures in Homophones Adventure 1

www.dovaspellingcity.com/aih1

CONTENTS

HOMOPHONES LIST 1

ail - To be sick; to trouble
ale - A type of beer

air - Atmosphere
heir - One who inherits

aisle - A passage way
isle - An island

all - The whole
awl - A shoemaker's tool

allowed - Granted; permitted
aloud - With noise; loudly

Word Maze Puzzle 1

Beginning with the circled letter, use the clues to find and mark the trail of letters of all the connected words through the maze to the last letter. The path can wander up, down, left, right, and diagonally.

Z	P	F	W	R	I	A	K	I	R	A	O	Z	V	K
B	C	P	X	D	F	T	G	A	L	W	J	J	Q	Z
H	G	D	Z	J	I	D	R	L	I	P	U	E	H	C
I	I	Z	L	(A)	C	F	L	E	A	E	F	A	F	D
S	A	L	O	U	D	I	S	A	L	L	W	Z	Y	Y
K	V	Q	Y	G	O	K	W	O	L	S	E	B	A	G
V	D	V	G	E	H	D	E	E	A	I	X	H	U	U
X	T	D	D	I	R	L	A	L	E	Q	T	D	N	D
N	M	I	E	T	A	L	E	Z	O	I	W	T	X	U
B	E	Z	E	C	I	L	C	D	B	E	B	E	G	R

1. With noise; loudly
2. An island
3. Granted; permitted
4. One who inherits
5. The whole

6. A type of beer
7. A passage way
8. To be sick; to trouble
9. Atmosphere
10. A shoemaker's tool

Jumbled Letters Quiz 1

The letters of the words below are jumbled. Figure out the word that best matches the clue:

Clue	Jumbled Letters	Answer
1. A type of beer	**ela**	_____
2. An island	**elsi**	_____
3. The whole	**lla**	_____
4. A passage way	**elsia**	_____
5. Granted; permitted	**dewolla**	_____
6. To be sick; to trouble	**lia**	_____
7. A shoemaker's tool	**lwa**	_____
8. With noise; loudly	**doula**	_____
9. Atmosphere	**ria**	_____
10. One who inherits	**rieh**	_____

Word Shapes Puzzle 1

Print the words from the list in the empty boxes. The shape of the word must match the shape of the boxes.

1.

6.

2.

7.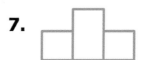

3.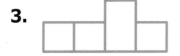

8.

4.

9.

5.

10.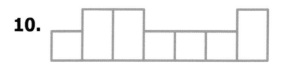

1. A passage way
2. Atmosphere
3. An island
4. The whole
5. With noise; loudly

6. To be sick; to trouble
7. A type of beer
8. One who inherits
9. A shoemaker's tool
10. Granted; permitted

Spelling Challenge Quiz 1

For each question below a number of similar words appear, but only one is spelled correctly and matches the clue that is provided. Give the letter of the correctly spelled word:

1. One who inherits   **A.** hier   **B.** air   **C.** ear   **D.** heir

2. With noise; loudly   **A.** aloud   **B.** allowed   **C.** alowed   **D.** alowd

3. A shoemaker's tool   **A.** aul   **B.** awll   **C.** awl   **D.** all

4. A type of beer   **A.** ial   **B.** ale   **C.** ail   **D.** ael

5. Atmosphere   **A.** heir   **B.** hier   **C.** ear   **D.** air

6. An island   **A.** iasle   **B.** aisle   **C.** isle   **D.** isel

7. The whole   **A.** all   **B.** aul   **C.** al   **D.** awl

8. To be sick; to trouble   **A.** ial   **B.** ail   **C.** ale   **D.** ael

9. A passage way   **A.** isle   **B.** asile   **C.** aisle   **D.** aesle

10. Granted; permitted   **A.** alowd   **B.** aloud   **C.** alowed   **D.** allowed

Alphabet Soup Puzzle 1

Each line of the puzzle has one word hidden in a list of random letters. The blank space is a missing letter that belongs to that word. Decide what word is hidden in the letters and write in the space the missing letter.

L	C	Y	R	G	A		E	Y	X	M	O	D
R	K	O	F	H	E		R	F	A	G	E	O
Z	I	A	U	A	L		O	W	E	D	Z	T
Y	B	T	I	S	L		W	H	H	I	T	F
M	Y	P	S	A	I		L	S	F	J	C	Z
U	Z	A	I	S	L		S	H	Y	B	M	Z
W	D	M	A	L	O		D	Y	E	G	B	G
T	B	R	Q	E	T		I	R	Z	G	R	D
P	J	P	L	B	A		L	T	M	A	N	I
O	H	Z	B	M	A		L	Z	A	J	F	A

1. A type of beer
2. One who inherits
3. Granted; permitted
4. An island
5. To be sick; to trouble

6. A passage way
7. With noise; loudly
8. Atmosphere
9. The whole
10. A shoemaker's tool

altar - A place for sacrifice or worship
alter - To change

ant - A small insect
aunt - The sister of your father or mother

ate - Past tense of eat
eight - One more than seven

bad - Not good
bade - Past tense of bid

bail - Surety; temporary release of an accused person awaiting trial
bail - A small piece of wood used in cricket
bale - A large bundle

Word Maze Puzzle 2

Beginning with the circled letter, use the clues to find and mark the trail of letters of all the connected words through the maze to the last letter. The path can wander up, down, left, right, and diagonally.

B	F	K	A	N	T	B	K	L	Y	Q	B	D	S	L
F	A	L	E	C	D	A	O	A	S	K	Y	H	A	R
C	(B)	T	L	A	E	T	I	L	J	S	N	S	C	I
P	R	A	T	H	G	R	C	M	O	U	V	G	A	P
U	A	A	B	E	I	I	P	R	C	E	C	M	P	A
N	L	I	A	D	M	U	Q	G	S	Y	M	C	Y	C
T	A	T	B	R	F	C	I	B	K	V	O	A	C	M
Y	P	E	R	E	H	L	J	N	C	F	H	G	G	X
R	Q	B	A	T	L	N	Y	L	J	N	C	R	W	E
U	M	Z	I	L	A	O	G	H	Q	C	K	D	C	X

1. A large bundle
2. A small insect
3. Past tense of bid
4. A place for sacrifice or worship
5. The sister of your father or mother
6. Past tense of eat

7. Surety; temporary release of an accused person awaiting trial
8. To change
9. Not good
10. One more than seven
11. A small piece of wood used in cricket

Jumbled Letters Quiz 2

The letters of the words below are jumbled. Figure out the word that best matches the clue:

Clue	Jumbled Letters	Answer
1. One more than seven	**thgie**	_____
2. Past tense of bid	**edab**	_____
3. A small piece of wood used in cricket	**liab**	_____
4. Past tense of eat	**eta**	_____
5. A place for sacrifice or worship	**ratla**	_____
6. A large bundle	**elab**	_____
7. To change	**retla**	_____
8. The sister of your father or mother	**tnua**	_____
9. A small insect	**tna**	_____
10. Not good	**dab**	_____

Word Shapes Puzzle 2

Print the words from the list in the empty boxes. The shape of the word must match the shape of the boxes.

1.

2.

3.

4.

5.

6.

7.

8.

9.

10.

11.

1. To change

2. A small piece of wood used in cricket

3. One more than seven

4. Not good

5. Surety; temporary release of an accused person awaiting trial

6. A large bundle

7. Past tense of eat

8. The sister of your father or mother

9. A place for sacrifice or worship

10. Past tense of bid

11. A small insect

Spelling Challenge Quiz 2

For each question below a number of similar words appear, but only one is spelled correctly and matches the clue that is provided. Give the letter of the correctly spelled word:

1. One more than seven   **A.** eat **B.** eight **C.** eighte **D.** ate

2. Past tense of eat   **A.** eight **B.** eat **C.** eighte **D.** ate

3. A small insect   **A.** anz **B.** ant **C.** ante **D.** aunt

4. A place for sacrifice or worship   **A.** altar **B.** alter **C.** altir **D.** altare

5. Past tense of bid   **A.** badde **B.** bade **C.** bide **D.** bad

6. To change   **A.** alter **B.** altre **C.** altir **D.** altar

7. A small piece of wood used in cricket   **A.** baile **B.** bail **C.** bael **D.** bale

8. Surety; temporary release of an accused

person awaiting trial   **A.** bail **B.** bale **C.** baile **D.** bael

9. The sister of your father or mother   **A.** aunt **B.** ante **C.** ant **D.** uant

10. A large bundle   **A.** baile **B.** bael **C.** bail **D.** bale

11. Not good   **A.** baid **B.** badd **C.** bade **D.** bad

Alphabet Soup Puzzle 2

Each line of the puzzle has one word hidden in a list of random letters. The blank space is a missing letter that belongs to that word. Decide what word is hidden in the letters and write in the space the missing letter.

U	H	A	N		N	O	J	E
B	E	J	B		D	O	J	R
H	A	A	T		W	S	K	F
U	N	J	E		G	H	T	D
F	C	B	A		L	Z	V	G
R	X	F	Z		U	N	T	H
B	B	A	D		Y	P	R	S
C	M	U	Y		L	T	E	R
R	F	B	A		E	K	B	T
F	R	M	E		L	T	A	R

1. A small insect
2. Not good
3. Past tense of eat
4. One more than seven
5. Surety; temporary release of an accused person awaiting trial

6. The sister of your father or mother
7. Past tense of bid
8. To change
9. A large bundle
10. A place for sacrifice or worship

baited - Past tense of bait
bated - Diminished or moderated

bald - Lacking hair
bawled - Shouted

ball - A round body; a formal dance
bawl - To cry loudly; to shout

baron - A title; a very wealthy or powerful businessman
barren - Desolate; unable to bear

bare - Uncovered; unfurnished; simple
bear - An animal; to endure
beer - A drink

Word Maze Puzzle 3

Beginning with the circled letter, use the clues to find and mark the trail of letters of all the connected words through the maze to the last letter. The path can wander up, down, left, right, and diagonally.

A	B	L	W	A	B	D	B	G	A	A	R	E	M	Z
W	R	W	I	W	F	L	R	L	Q	(B)	A	B	R	N
L	B	M	L	Y	K	A	C	N	R	A	G	E	D	I
E	D	J	G	O	E	B	D	Z	Z	B	R	E	G	G
D	G	G	U	L	Q	X	E	R	I	A	P	V	K	K
R	B	Y	D	W	M	Z	T	I	A	L	T	J	A	G
V	J	T	Y	P	Q	N	A	R	B	L	L	R	L	H
U	F	Q	N	U	E	V	B	O	N	B	E	A	I	L
K	S	X	M	I	I	E	D	L	E	R	B	R	H	N
Z	M	W	G	A	Z	T	A	B	N	R	A	C	W	Y

1. Uncovered; unfurnished; simple
2. A drink
3. A round body; a formal dance
4. An animal; to endure
5. Desolate; unable to bear
6. Diminished or moderated

7. A very wealthy or powerful businessman; a title
8. Past tense of bait
9. Lacking hair
10. To cry loudly; to shout
11. Shouted; cried loudly

Jumbled Letters Quiz 3

The letters of the words below are jumbled. Figure out the word that best matches the clue:

Clue	Jumbled Letters	Answer
1. A very wealthy or powerful businessman	norab	_____
2. Desolate; unable to bear	nerrab	_____
3. To cry loudly; to shout	lwab	_____
4. A round body	llab	_____
5. A title	norab	_____
6. Diminished or moderated	detab	_____
7. An animal	raeb	_____
8. Shouted	delwab	_____
9. Past tense of bait	detiab	_____
10. To endure	raeb	_____
11. Lacking hair	dlab	_____
12. Unfurnished; simple	erab	_____
13. A formal dance	llab	_____
14. A drink	reeb	_____

Word Shapes Puzzle 3

Print the words from the list in the empty boxes. The shape of the word must match the shape of the boxes.

1.

2.

3.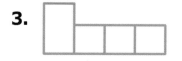

4.

5.

6.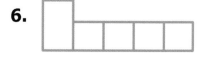

7.

8.

9.

10.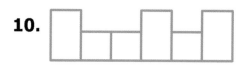

11.

1. An animal; to endure
2. Desolate; unable to bear
3. Uncovered; unfurnished; simple
4. Lacking hair
5. A drink
6. A very wealthy or powerful businessman; a title

7. To cry loudly; to shout
8. A round body; a formal dance
9. Past tense of bait
10. Shouted; cried loudly
11. Diminished or moderated

Spelling Challenge Quiz 3

For each question below a number of similar words appear, but only one is spelled correctly and matches the clue that is provided. Give the letter of the correctly spelled word:

1. A drink

A. beir **B.** bear **C.** bare **D.** beer

2. Past tense of bait

A. baeted **B.** baited **C.** biated **D.** bated

3. A formal dance

A. balle **B.** ball **C.** baul **D.** bawl

4. A title

A. baren **B.** barin **C.** baron **D.** barron

5. To cry loudly; to shout

A. bawle **B.** bawl **C.** ball **D.** baul

6. An animal

A. bear **B.** beer **C.** bare **D.** bere

7. Lacking hair

A. bald **B.** bawld **C.** bawled **D.** bauld

8. Diminished or moderated

A. baited **B.** batted **C.** bated **D.** batede

9. Uncovered; unfurnished; simple

A. bare **B.** bere **C.** beer **D.** bear

10. Shouted

A. bald **B.** bawlled **C.** bawled **D.** bawld

11. To endure

A. bare **B.** bere **C.** beer **D.** bear

12. A round body

A. bahl **B.** ball **C.** bal **D.** bawl

13. A very wealthy or powerful businessman

A. barone **B.** byron **C.** baren **D.** baron

14. Desolate; unable to bear

A. baron **B.** barren **C.** barron **D.** baren

Alphabet Soup Puzzle 3

Each line of the puzzle has one word hidden in a list of random letters. The blank space is a missing letter that belongs to that word. Decide what word is hidden in the letters and write in the space the missing letter.

D	C	B	D	O		A	I	T	E	D
G	Y	D	B	A		E	K	H	J	X
H	V	B	A	R		N	G	M	Z	K
D	R	T	L	B		A	R	C	J	M
T	K	W	M	B		R	R	E	N	Q
G	M	P	I	S		A	L	D	X	G
B	E	M	B	A		L	E	D	I	C
T	U	L	P	P		A	L	L	B	A
K	X	B	E	E		H	X	M	J	A
E	T	H	Y	G		A	W	L	H	Z
C	Y	V	B	A		E	D	Q	V	W

1. Past tense of bait
2. Uncovered; unfurnished; simple
3. A very wealthy or powerful businessman; a title
4. An animal; to endure
5. Desolate; unable to bear

6. Lacking hair
7. Shouted; cried loudly
8. A round body; a formal dance
9. A drink
10. To cry loudly; to shout
11. Diminished or moderated

18

base - A place from which an army operates; the lowest part
bass - The lowest part of a musical range; a type of fish

be - To exist
bee - An insect

beach - A seashore
beech - A kind of tree

bean - A kidney-shaped seed
been - Past participle of be

beat - Regular route of a police officer; a rhythm
beat - To strike repeatedly; to overcome
beet - A vegetable

Word Maze Puzzle 4

Beginning with the circled letter, use the clues to find and mark the trail of letters of all the connected words through the maze to the last letter. The path can wander up, down, left, right, and diagonally.

M	C	Q	B	A	V	W	V	W	Y	B	D	W	E	M
V	Y	G	D	Y	C	B	I	F	Y	B	E	Q	X	W
C	A	Q	N	I	A	U	U	E	B	M	E	Q	K	V
I	B	G	S	A	H	C	T	E	E	G	S	J	D	J
Y	Q	K	U	K	D	E	B	Y	B	T	A	Q	F	X
A	V	A	M	I	B	E	E	V	M	B	E	B	D	T
Z	I	S	F	A	H	C	A	A	S	S	E	S	J	D
K	F	M	Z	R	S	E	A	B	B	N	E	X	X	G
J	Q	N	N	L	N	(B)	N	E	E	V	E	M	A	T
J	F	T	R	F	J	K	B	A	S	E	B	Q	Y	F

1. A kidney-shaped seed

2. A place from which an army operates; the lowest part

3. Past participle of be

4. An insect

5. The lowest part of a musical range; a type of fish

6. To strike repeatedly; to overcome

7. To exist

8. A vegetable

9. A seashore

10. A kind of tree

Jumbled Letters Quiz 4

The letters of the words below are jumbled. Figure out the word that best matches the clue:

Clue	Jumbled Letters	Answer
1. A type of fish	ssab	_____
2. To exist	eb	_____
3. A kind of tree	hceeb	_____
4. A kidney-shaped seed	naeb	_____
5. A place from which an army operates	esab	_____
6. Regular route of a police officer	taeb	_____
7. Lowest part of a musical range	ssab	_____
8. A rhythm	taeb	_____
9. Past participle of be	neeb	_____
10. A seashore	hcaeb	_____
11. A vegetable	teeb	_____
12. To overcome	taeb	_____
13. An insect	eeb	_____
14. The lowest part	esab	_____

Word Shapes Puzzle 4

Print the words from the list in the empty boxes. The shape of the word must match the shape of the boxes.

1.

2.

3.

4.

5.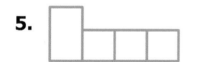

6.

7.

8.

9.

10.

1. Past participle of be

2. To strike repeatedly; to overcome

3. A place from which an army operates; the lowest part

4. A kind of tree

5. The lowest part of a musical range; a type of fish

6. A vegetable

7. An insect

8. A kidney-shaped seed

9. To exist

10. A seashore

Spelling Challenge Quiz 4

For each question below a number of similar words appear, but only one is spelled correctly and matches the clue that is provided. Give the letter of the correctly spelled word

1. An insect   **A.** bee   **B.** bie   **C.** be   **D.** b

2. A kind of tree   **A.** byech   **B.** beach   **C.** baech   **D.** beech

3. A place from which an army

operates   **A.** base   **B.** bass   **C.** basse   **D.** bas

4. Past participle of be   **A.** beane   **B.** bean   **C.** been   **D.** bene

5. A seashore   **A.** beich   **B.** beach   **C.** baech   **D.** beech

6. A type of fish   **A.** bace   **B.** base   **C.** bass   **D.** bas

7. The lowest part of a musical range   **A.** base   **B.** bas   **C.** basse   **D.** bass

8. To exist   **A.** bie   **B.** be   **C.** bee   **D.** eb

9. The lowest part   **A.** basse   **B.** base   **C.** bass   **D.** bace

10. To strike repeatedly; to overcome   **A.** beat   **B.** beet   **C.** beit   **D.** bete

11. Regular route of a police officer   **A.** beit   **B.** beet   **C.** beat   **D.** biet

12. A rhythm   **A.** beat   **B.** beet   **C.** bete   **D.** beit

13. A vegetable   **A.** beat   **B.** beit   **C.** beet   **D.** bete

14. A kidney-shaped seed   **A.** bein   **B.** bene   **C.** bean   **D.** been

Alphabet Soup Puzzle 4

Each line of the puzzle has one word hidden in a list of random letters. The blank space is a missing letter that belongs to that word. Decide what word is hidden in the letters and write in the space the missing letter.

L	J	L	X		E	E	T	K
X	F	R	E		E	A	K	N
S	P	B	B		E	N	I	Z
B	E	E	C		L	F	X	G
M	B	A	S		C	P	I	O
J	V	K	M		A	S	E	Q
B	I	L	O		E	E	T	O
B	E	A	C		G	Z	F	U
W	X	B	E		T	Q	G	T
S	B	E	A		C	C	J	C

1. An insect
2. To exist
3. Past participle of be
4. A kind of tree
5. The lowest part of a musical range; a type of fish

6. A place from which an army operates; the lowest part
7. A vegetable
8. A seashore
9. To strike repeatedly; to overcome
10. A kidney-shaped seed

.

HOMOPHONES LIST 5

beau - A woman's male friend
bow - A knot with two loops and loose ends; a weapon

bell - A hollow-sounding metallic vessel; a signal
belle - A beautiful girl or woman

berry - A small fruit
bury - To cover; to conceal; hide

berth - A resting place; a room in a ship
birth - The act of coming to life

blew - Past tense of blow
blue - A colour

Word Maze Puzzle 5

Beginning with the circled letter, use the clues to find and mark the trail of letters of all the connected words through the maze to the last letter. The path can wander up, down, left, right, and diagonally.

P	Q	G	Y	J	T	I	Y	Z	R	R	R	T	H	B
V	R	J	P	J	A	H	M	V	I	B	E	I	B	E
N	W	V	M	Y	W	B	C	S	E	W	T	R	L	L
R	L	W	Q	C	J	N	D	M	L	B	H	R	C	W
I	T	B	N	E	P	F	C	N	C	U	A	E	D	D
B	U	L	L	L	W	H	W	G	Z	F	E	R	R	Y
B	H	F	W	W	V	U	T	L	L	E	B	Y	E	L
F	C	U	Y	T	H	V	A	E	B	B	O	W	B	E
P	H	T	M	A	O	C	R	A	E	U	L	B	Y	Ⓑ
V	V	A	B	U	V	P	D	H	Z	G	R	G	R	U

1. To cover; to conceal; hide
2. A colour
3. A beautiful girl or woman
4. A knot with two loops and loose ends
5. A small fruit
6. A woman's male friend
7. Past tense of blow
8. A resting place; a room in a ship
9. A hollow-sounding metallic vessel; a signal
10. The act of coming to life

Jumbled Letters Quiz 5

The letters of the words below are jumbled. Figure out the word that best matches the clue:

Clue	Jumbled Letters	Answer
1. A knot with two loops and loose ends	**wob**	_____
2. The act of coming to life	**htrib**	_____
3. A beautiful girl or woman	**elleb**	_____
4. To cover; to conceal; hide	**yrub**	_____
5. A hollow-sounding metallic vessel; a signal	**lleb**	_____
6. Past tense of blow	**welb**	_____
7. A woman's male friend	**uaeb**	_____
8. A resting place; a room in a ship	**htreb**	_____
9. A small fruit	**yrreb**	_____
10. A colour	**eulb**	_____
11. A weapon	**wob**	_____

Word Shapes Puzzle 5

Print the words from the list in the empty boxes. The shape of the word must match the shape of the boxes.

1.

6.

2.

7.

3.

8.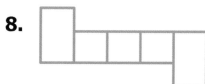

4.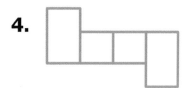

9.

5.

10.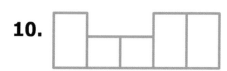

1. The act of coming to life
2. Past tense of blow
3. A colour
4. To cover; to conceal; hide
5. A knot with two loops and loose ends
6. A woman's male friend

7. A beautiful girl or woman
8. A small fruit
9. A hollow-sounding metallic vessel; a signal
10. A resting place; a room in a ship

Spelling Challenge Quiz 5

For each question below a number of similar words appear, but only one is spelled correctly and matches the clue that is provided. Give the letter of the correctly spelled word:

1. A hollow-sounding metallic vessel; a

signal **A.** belle **B.** bell **C.** bel **D.** bele

2. Past tense of blow **A.** blu **B.** bleu **C.** blew **D.** blue

3. A small fruit **A.** bury **B.** bery **C.** berry **D.** burry

4. A colour **A.** blue **B.** blu **C.** bleu **D.** blew

5. A woman's male friend **A.** beau **B.** baeu **C.** bow **D.** bowe

6. A beautiful girl or woman **A.** bele **B.** bel **C.** bell **D.** belle

7. The act of coming to life **A.** burth **B.** birthe **C.** birth **D.** berth

8. To cover; to conceal; hide **A.** buri **B.** bury **C.** berry **D.** burry

9. A resting place; a room in a ship **A.** berth **B.** birth **C.** berthe **D.** burth

10. A weapon **A.** boe **B.** bowe **C.** bow **D.** bou

11. A knot with two loops and loose

ends **A.** bo **B.** bow **C.** beau **D.** bowe

Alphabet Soup Puzzle 5

Each line of the puzzle has one word hidden in a list of random letters. The blank space is a missing letter that belongs to that word. Decide what word is hidden in the letters and write in the space the missing letter.

I	E	L	H		O	W	Z	D
E	R	D	M		U	R	Y	W
L	C	L	B		U	E	P	A
N	J	B	E		L	E	H	Y
C	M	V	Q		E	R	T	H
R	V	L	B		E	W	N	L
A	F	B	E		L	F	L	J
Z	B	O	B		R	T	H	F
K	B	E	R		Y	H	R	V
G	S	Z	T		E	A	U	N

1. A knot with two loops and loose ends
2. To cover; to conceal; hide
3. A colour
4. A beautiful girl or woman
5. A resting place; a room in a ship
6. Past tense of blow

7. A hollow-sounding metallic vessel; a signal
8. The act of coming to life
9. A small fruit
10. A woman's male friend

HOMOPHONES VOCABULARY BUILDER LIST 1

ail - To be sick; to trouble
ale - A type of beer

air - Atmosphere
heir - One who inherits

aisle - A passage way
isle - An island

all - The whole
awl - A shoemaker's tool

allowed - Granted; permitted
aloud - With noise; loudly

altar - A place for sacrifice or worship
alter - To change

ant - A small insect
aunt - The sister of your father or mother

ate - Past tense of eat
eight - One more than seven

bad - Not good
bade - Past tense of bid

bail - Surety; temporary release of an accused person awaiting trial
bail - A small piece of wood used in cricket
bale - A large bundle

baited - Past tense of bait
bated - Diminished or moderated

bald - Lacking hair
bawled - Shouted

ball - A round body
ball - A formal dance
bawl - To cry loudly; to shout

baron - A title
baron - A very wealthy or powerful businessman
barren - Desolate; unable to bear

bare - Uncovered; unfurnished; simple
bear - An animal
bear - To endure
beer - A drink

base - The lowest part
base - A place from which an army operates
bass - The lowest part of a musical range
bass - A type of fish

be - To exist
bee - An insect

beach - A seashore
beech - A kind of tree

bean - A kidney-shaped seed
been - Past participle of be

beat - Regular route of a police officer
beat - A rhythm
beat - To strike repeatedly; to overcome
beet - A vegetable

beau - A woman's male friend
bow - A weapon
bow - A knot with two loops and loose ends

bell - A hollow-sounding metallic vessel; a signal
belle - A beautiful girl or woman

berry - A small fruit
bury - To cover; to conceal; hide

berth - A resting place; a room in a ship
birth - The act of coming to life

blew - Past tense of blow
blue - A colour

REVIEW EXERCISE 1

Underline the word that best matches each clue:

1. The lowest part   (base, bass)

2. One who inherits   (air, heir)

3. A small fruit   (berry, bury)

4. Diminished or moderated   (bated, baited)

5. A formal dance   (ball, bawl)

6. An insect   (be, bee)

7. A passage way   (aisle, isle)

8. A weapon   (beau, bow)

9. Past tense of bid   (bad, bade)

10. Atmosphere   (air, heir)

11. A knot with two loops and loose ends   (beau, bow)

12. A resting place; a room in a ship   (berth, birth)

13. Uncovered; unfurnished; simple   (bare, bear, beer)

14. The act of coming to life   (berth, birth)

15. A woman's male friend   (beau, bow)

16. A large bundle   (bail, bale)

17. To strike repeatedly; to overcome   (beat, beet)

18. A beautiful girl or woman   (bell, belle)

19. To cry loudly; to shout   (ball, bawl)

20. A type of fish   (base, bass)

21. A title   **(baron, barren)**

22. A vegetable   **(beat, beet)**

23. The lowest part of a musical range   **(base, bass)**

24. A seashore   **(beach, beech)**

25. To change   **(altar, alter)**

26. Shouted   **(bald, bawled)**

27. An island   **(aisle, isle)**

28. A small piece of wood used in cricket   **(bail, bale)**

29. Lacking hair   **(bald, bawled)**

30. The whole   **(all, awl)**

31. One more than seven   **(ate, eight)**

32. Regular route of a police officer   **(beat, beet)**

33. Past tense of eat   **(ate, eight)**

34. An animal   **(bare, bear, beer)**

35. A kidney-shaped seed   **(bean, been)**

36. A type of beer   **(ail, ale)**

37. To cover; to conceal; hide   **(berry, bury)**

38. A round body   **(ball, bawl)**

39. A very wealthy or powerful businessman   **(baron, barren)**

40. With noise; loudly   **(allowed, aloud)**

41. Past tense of bait   **(bated, baited)**

42. To exist   **(be, bee)**

43. To endure   **(bare, bear, beer)**

44. A colour   **(blew, blue)**

45. A rhythm   **(beat, beet)**

46. Surety; temporary release of an accused person awaiting trial (bail, bale)

47. A shoemaker's tool (all, awl)

48. A small insect (ant, aunt)

49. A kind of tree (beach, beech)

50. Not good (bad, bade)

51. To be sick; to trouble (ail, ale)

52. A place for sacrifice or worship (altar, alter)

53. The sister of your father or mother (ant, aunt)

54. Granted; permitted (allowed, aloud)

55. A hollow-sounding metallic vessel; a signal (bell, belle)

56. A drink (bare, bear, beer)

57. Desolate; unable to bear (baron, barren)

58. Past participle of be (bean, been)

59. Past tense of blow (blew, blue)

REVIEW EXERCISE 2

There are letters missing in each word below. Give the complete word that best matches the clue:

Clue	Missing Letters	Answer
1. Shouted	b _ wl _ d	_____
2. To change	_ lt _ r	_____
3. Past tense of blow	bl _ w	_____
4. Atmosphere	_ _ r	_____
5. A knot with two loops and loose ends	b _ w	_____
6. A beautiful girl or woman	b _ ll _	_____
7. A drink	b _ _ r	_____
8. The whole	_ ll	_____
9. A vegetable	b _ _ t	_____
10. To strike repeatedly; to overcome	b _ _ t	_____
11. The sister of your father or mother	_ _ nt	_____
12. A shoemaker's tool	_ wl	_____
13. Desolate; unable to bear	b _ rr _ n	_____
14. Surety; temporary release of an accused person awaiting trial	b _ _ l	_____

Clue	Missing Letters	Answer
15. Granted; permitted	_ ll _ w _ d	_____
16. An insect	b _ _	_____
17. A round body	b _ ll	_____
18. One more than seven	_ _ ght	_____
19. Diminished or moderated	b _ t _ d	_____
20. A place for sacrifice or worship	_ lt _ r	_____
21. An island	_ sl _	_____
22. Past tense of eat	_ t _	_____
23. Regular route of a police officer	b _ _ t	_____
24. Past tense of bait	b _ _ t _ d	_____
25. A woman's male friend	b _ _ _	_____
26. With noise; loudly	_ l _ _ d	_____
27. To exist	b _	_____
28. A title	b _ r _ n	_____
29. Lacking hair	b _ ld	_____
30. A kind of tree	b _ _ ch	_____
31. A very wealthy or powerful businessman	b _ r _ n	_____
32. To be sick; to trouble	_ _ l	_____
33. The lowest part of a musical range	b _ ss	_____

Clue	Missing Letters	Answer
34. A place from which an army operates	b _ s _	_____
35. A small fruit	b _ rry	_____
36. A small insect	_ nt	_____
37. To endure	b _ _ r	_____
38. A hollow-sounding metallic vessel; a signal	b _ ll	_____
39. The act of coming to life	b _ rth	_____
40. A resting place; a room in a ship	b _ rth	_____
41. A formal dance	b _ ll	_____
42. Past participle of be	b _ _ n	_____
43. One who inherits	h _ _ r	_____
44. An animal	b _ _ r	_____
45. A large bundle	b _ l _	_____
46. A seashore	b _ _ ch	_____
47. To cry loudly; to shout	b _ wl	_____
48. Past tense of bid	b _ d _	_____
49. The lowest part	b _ s _	_____
50. A colour	bl _ _	_____
51. A rhythm	b _ _ t	_____
52. A kidney-shaped seed	b _ _ n	_____
53. A type of fish	b _ ss	_____
54. A weapon	b _ w	_____

Clue	Missing Letters	Answer
55. Uncovered; unfurnished; simple	b _ r _	_____
56. A passage way	_ _ sl _	_____
57. Not good	b _ d	_____
58. To cover; to conceal; hide	b _ ry	_____
59. A type of beer	_ l _	_____
60. A small piece of wood used in cricket	b _ _ l	_____

.

Underline the word that best matches each clue:

1. If you drink that **(ale, ail)** you will **(ale, ail)**.

2. The young **(air, heir)** sought shelter from the cold **(air, heir)**.

3. The **(aisle, isle)** of the church in the **(Aisle, Isle)** of Man is not as long as this one.

4. **(All, Awl)** the poor shoemaker owned was an **(all, awl)**.

5. You are not **(allowed, aloud)** to read **(allowed, aloud)** in the library.

6. His manner did not **(altar, alter)** when he stood before the **(altar, alter)**.

7. My **(ant, aunt)** was stung by an **(ant, aunt)** on her great toe.

8. The greedy boy **(eight, ate)(eight, ate)** pies.

9. His father **(bad, bade)** him to avoid **(bad, bade)** company.

10. **(Bail, Bale)** was refused for the person that stole the **(bail, bale)** of silk.

11. They watched with **(baited, bated)** breath as the man they had **(baited, bated)** approached.

12. He **(bald, bawled)** so loudly that old man Joe popped his **(bald, bawled)** head out of the window.

13. He began to **(ball, bawl)** when the **(ball, bawl)** struck him.

14. The **(baron, barren)** wept when he saw the **(baron, barren)** land.

15. After he drank **(bare, bear, beer)** the man tried to beat the grizzly **(bare, bear, beer)** with his **(bare, bear, beer)** hands.

16. (Be, Bee) diligent like the busy **(be, bee)**.

17. With some dried limbs of the dead **(beach, beech)** tree they made a fire on the sandy **(beach, beech)**.

18. The man with the **(base, bass)** voice stood at the **(base, bass)** of the mountain.

19. When Jack ate the **(bean, been)** it had already **(bean, been)** on the table for three days.

20. The clown tried to **(beat, beet)** the **(beat, beet)** root with a stick while dancing to the **(beat, beet)** of calypso music.

21. Her **(beau, bow)** was shot with an arrow from a **(beau, bow)**.

22. The **(bell, belle)** walked up to the door and rang the **(bell, belle)**.

23. If you **(berry, bury)** that **(berry, bury)** it will grow.

24. The poor sailor was confined to his **(berth, birth)** by sickness during his **(berth, birth)**-day.

25. The wind **(blew, blue)** the **(blew, blue)** flag.

borough - A town with its own local government
burrow - A hole made by an animal

brute - A cruel, violent person
bruit - Tell or spread rumours

but - However; despite this
butt - The thick end of a weapon

buy - To purchase
by – Near
bye - A farewell remark
bye - A run scored in cricket

cannon - A large heavy gun
canon - A priest; a general rule

Volume 2 List 3 Spiral Puzzle

Numbered clues appear below the spiral grid. Determine the word that matches the clue, and write that word in the spiral puzzle. The word does not overlap with the next word (marked by the next number) and it must be written in the correct direction (from a lower numbered space to a higher numbered space).

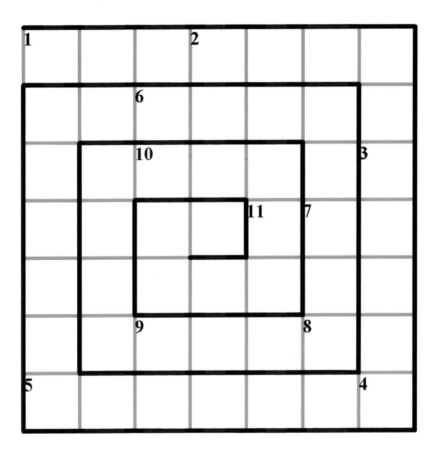

1. To purchase
2. Tell or spread rumours
3. The thick end of a tool or weapon
4. A hole or tunnel made by an animal
5. A town with its own local government
6. A cruel, violent person

7. Near
8. A farewell remark; a run scored in cricket
9. A priest; a general rule
10. However; despite this
11. A large heavy gun

Volume 2 List 3 Matching Quiz

Provide the word that best matches each clue.

1. _____   A priest; a general rule

2. _____   However; despite this

3. _____   A town with its own local government

4. _____   A cruel, violent person

5. _____   A large heavy gun

6. _____   A farewell remark

7. _____   Tell or spread rumours

8. _____   Near

9. _____   The thick end of a weapon

10. _____   To purchase

11. _____   A hole made by an animal

A. bruit   **B.** buy   **C.** but   **D.** by   **E.** cannon   **F.** bye

G. burrow   **H.** butt   **I.** canon   **J.** brute   **K.** borough

Volume 2 List 3 Crossword Puzzle

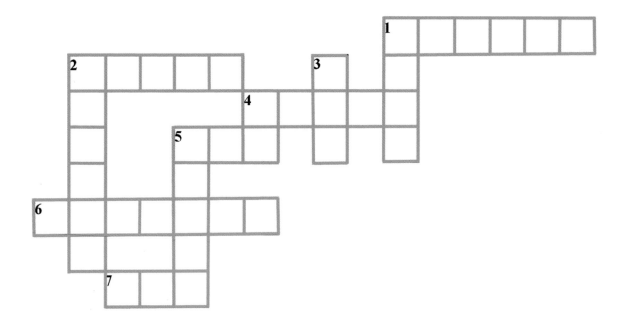

ACROSS

1. A hole or tunnel made by an animal

2. A priest; a general rule

4. Tell or spread rumours

5. To purchase

6. A town with its own local government

7. A farewell remark; a run scored in cricket

DOWN

1. The thick end of a tool or weapon

2. A large heavy gun

3. However; despite this

4. Near

5. A cruel, violent person

Volume 2 List 3 Spelling Challenge Quiz

For each question below a number of similar words appear, but only one is spelled correctly and matches the clue that is provided. Give the letter of the correctly spelled word:

1. The thick end of a weapon   **A.** but   **B.** bot   **C.** bott   **D.** butt

2. Near   **A.** by   **B.** bye   **C.** bie   **D.** buy

3. A cruel, violent person   **A.** brute   **B.** bruit   **C.** bruite   **D.** brut

4. A run scored in cricket   **A.** buy   **B.** bie   **C.** bye   **D.** by

5. To purchase   **A.** buy   **B.** bye   **C.** bie   **D.** by

6. A town with its own local

government   **A.** burough   **B.** borough   **C.** burrow   **D.** burow

7. A farewell remark   **A.** by   **B.** buy   **C.** bye   **D.** bie

8. A priest; a general rule   **A.** kanon   **B.** canone   **C.** canon   **D.** cannon

9. A hole made by an animal   **A.** borough   **B.** birrow   **C.** burrow   **D.** burow

10. A large heavy gun   **A.** canon   **B.** kannon   **C.** cannon   **D.** canone

11. Tell or spread rumours   **A.** bruit   **B.** brute   **C.** bruite   **D.** brut

12. However; despite this   **A.** but   **B.** butt   **C.** bot   **D.** bott

Volume 2 List 3 Decoding Puzzle

The words below have been written in code. Use the hints in the decoder at the top of the page to help break the code (the letters on top are the correct answers, the numbers on the bottom are the code). Write the correct word on the line provided beside each code word.

1	2	3	4	5	6	7	8	9	10	11	12	13
14	15	16	17	18	19	20	21	22	23	24	25	26

1. 2-11 _____

2. 2-7-9-12-21 _____

3. 2-11-8 _____

4. 5-16-15-15-19-15 _____

5. 5-16-15-19-15 _____

6. 2-7-9-21-8 _____

7. 2-9-21 _____

8. 2-9-7-7-19-24 _____

9. 2-9-11 _____

10. 2-19-7-19-9-18-25 _____

11. 2-9-21-21 _____

1. Near
2. Tell or spread rumours
3. A farewell remark; a run scored in cricket
4. A large heavy gun
5. A priest; a general rule

6. A cruel, violent person
7. However; despite this
8. A hole or tunnel made by an animal
9. To purchase
10. A town with its own local government
11. The thick end of a tool or weapon

Dear Parents,

We hope that you enjoyed using *Teach Your Child: Homophones Vocabulary Builder 1 – Mobile Learning Help for Active Parents* as much as we enjoyed choosing and putting together the games, puzzles and quizzes in this book.

The activities that made it were the ones that we felt you would like. You can however help to choose which activities make it into future volumes in this series by indicating which activities you prefer when you review this book at Amazon.

This book is also available for your reading devices (kindle, computer, tablet, smartphone or iPad) at Amazon.

If you would like all of the lists in this and other volumes in one handy guide, **"Teach Your Child: Homophones Vocabulary Builder Parent's Reference"** is perfect for you.

You can always find the latest information about our books and future publications at: **www.DovaSpellingCity.com/bks** or **scan the QR code on the next page**.

In addition you may request **free resources** to accelerate your child's learning at: www.DovaSpellingCity.com/hftr1 or scan the QR code on the next page.

One last thing: Remember to get Volume 2.

Thank you and we wish you and your ward continued success as you *"Teach Your Child... and Yourself"*.

In gratitude,

The Dova Team

For Dova Spelling City
www.dovaspellingcity.com

Other Books by Dova Spelling City

www.DovaSpellingCity.com/bks

Request Your Free Resources

www.DovaSpellingCity.com/hftr1

Adventures in Homophones

Would your protégé prefer to learn this list using an interactive game?

Adventures in Homophones is ideal for the active parent and child. It is an online game that you can also download to your iPad.

After download your ward can use it **without** an internet connection.

Preview Adventures in Homophones 1 here: www.dovaspellingcity.com/aih1 or **scan the QR code below:**

Word Maze Puzzle 1 Solution

Z	P	F	W	R	I	A	K	R	A	O	Z	V	K
B	C	P	X	D	F	T	G	A	W	J	J	Q	Z
H	G	D	Z	J	I	D	R	L	P	U	E	H	C
I	I	Z	L	A	C	F	L	E	E	F	A	F	D
S	A	L	O	U	D	I	S	A	L	W	Z	Y	Y
K	V	Q	Y	G	O	K	W	O	S	E	B	A	G
V	D	V	G	E	H	D	E	E	A	X	H	U	U
X	T	D	D	I	R	L	A	E	Q	T	D	N	D
N	M	I	E	T	A	L	E	Z	O	I	W	T	X	U
B	E	Z	E	C	I	L	C	D	B	E	B	E	G	R

Jumbled Letters Quiz 1 Answers

1. ale **2.** isle **3.** all **4.** aisle **5.** allowed **6.** ail **7.** awl **8.** aloud **9.** air **10.** heir

Word Shapes Puzzle 1 Solution

1. a i s l e

2. a i r

3. i s l e

4. a l l

5. a l o u d

6. a i l

7. a l e

8. h e i r

9. a w l

10. a l l o w e d

52

Spelling Challenge Quiz 1 Answers

1. D **2.** A **3.** C **4.** B **5.** D **6.** C **7.** A **8.** B **9.** C **10.** D

Alphabet Soup Puzzle 1 Solution

L	C	Y	R	G	A	L	E	Y	X	M	O	D
R	K	O	F	H	E	I	R	F	A	G	E	O
Z	I	A	U	A	L	L	O	W	E	D	Z	T
Y	B	T	I	S	L	E	W	H	H	I	T	F
M	Y	P	S	A	I	L	L	S	F	J	C	Z
U	Z	A	I	S	L	E	S	H	Y	B	M	Z
W	D	M	A	L	O	U	D	Y	E	G	B	G
T	B	R	Q	E	T	A	I	R	Z	G	R	D
P	J	P	L	B	A	L	L	T	M	A	N	I
O	H	Z	B	M	A	W	L	Z	A	J	F	A

Word Maze Puzzle 2 Solution

B	F	K	A	N	T	B	K	L	Y	Q	B	D	S	L
F	A	L	E	C	D	A	O	A	S	K	Y	H	A	R
C	B	T	L	A	E	T	I	L	J	S	N	S	C	I
P	R	A	T	H	G	R	C	M	O	U	V	G	A	P
U	A	A	B	E	I	P	R	C	E	C	M	P	A	
N	L	A	D	M	U	Q	G	S	Y	M	C	Y	C	
T	A	T	B	R	F	C	I	B	K	V	O	A	C	M
Y	P	E	R	E	H	L	J	N	C	F	H	G	G	X
R	Q	B	A	T	L	N	Y	L	J	N	C	R	W	E
U	M	Z	L	A	O	G	H	Q	C	K	D	C	X	

Jumbled Letters Quiz 2 Answers

1. eight **2.** bade **3.** bail **4.** ate **5.** altar **6.** bale **7.** alter **8.** aunt **9.** ant **10.** bad

Word Shapes Puzzle 2 Solution

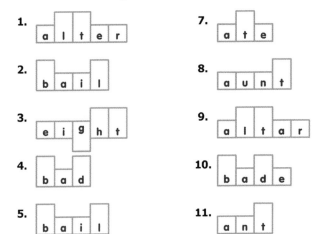

1. alter
2. bail
3. eight
4. bad
5. bail
6. bale
7. ate
8. aunt
9. altar
10. bade
11. ant

Spelling Challenge Quiz 2 Answers

1. B **2.** D **3.** B **4.** A **5.** B **6.** A **7.** B **8.** A **9.** A **10.** D **11.** D

Alphabet Soup Puzzle 2

Word Maze Puzzle 3 Solution

A	B	L	W	A	B	D	B	G	A	A	R	E	M	Z

(Word maze grid)

A	B	L	W	A	B	D	B	G	A	A	R	E	M	Z
W	R	W	I	W	F	L	R	L	Q	B	A	B	R	N
L	B	M	L	Y	K	A	C	N	R	A	G	E	D	I
E	D	J	G	O	E	B	D	Z	Z	B	R	E	G	G
D	G	G	U	L	Q	X	E	R	I	A	P	V	K	K
R	B	Y	D	W	M	Z	T	I	A	L	T	J	A	G
V	J	T	Y	P	Q	N	A	R	B	L	L	R	L	H
U	F	Q	N	U	E	V	B	O	N	B	E	A	I	L
K	S	X	M	I	I	E	D	L	E	R	B	R	H	N
Z	M	W	G	A	Z	T	A	B	N	R	A	C	W	Y

Jumbled Letters Quiz 3 Answers

1. baron **2.** barren **3.** bawl **4.** ball **5.** baron **6.** bated **7.** bear **8.** bawled **9.** baited

10. bear **11.** bald **12.** bare **13.** ball **14.** beer

Word Shapes Puzzle 3 Solution

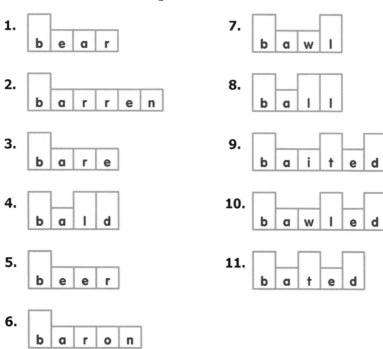

1. b e a r

2. b a r r e n

3. b a r e

4. b a l d

5. b e e r

6. b a r o n

7. b a w l

8. b a l l

9. b a i t e d

10. b a w l e d

11. b a t e d

Spelling Challenge Quiz 3 Answers

1. D **2.** B **3.** B **4.** C **5.** B **6.** A **7.** A **8.** C **9.** A **10.** C **11.** D **12.** B **13.** D **14.** B

Alphabet Soup Puzzle 3 Solution

D	C	B	D	O	B	A	I	T	E	D
G	Y	D	B	A	R	E	K	H	J	X
H	V	B	A	R	O	N	G	M	Z	K
D	R	T	L	B	E	A	R	C	J	M
T	K	W	M	B	A	R	R	E	N	Q
G	M	P	I	S	B	A	L	D	X	G
B	E	M	B	A	W	L	E	D	I	C
T	U	L	P	P	B	A	L	L	B	A
K	X	B	E	E	R	H	X	M	J	A
E	T	H	Y	G	B	A	W	L	H	Z
C	Y	V	B	A	T	E	D	Q	V	W

Word Maze Puzzle 4 Solution

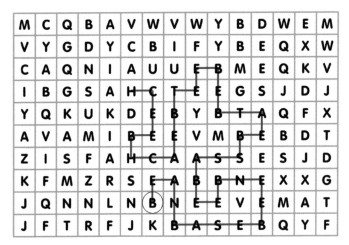

Jumbled Letters Quiz 4 Answers

1. bass **2.** be **3.** beech **4.** bean **5.** base **6.** beat **7.** bass **8.** beat **9.** been **10.** beach

11. beet **12.** beat **13.** bee **14.** base

Word Shapes Puzzle 4 Solution

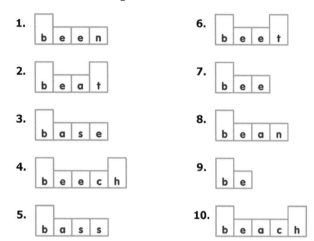

1. b e e n   **6.** b e e t

2. b e a t   **7.** b e e

3. b a s e   **8.** b e a n

4. b e e c h   **9.** b e

5. b a s s   **10.** b e a c h

Spelling Challenge Quiz 4 Answers

1. A **2.** D **3.** A **4.** C **5.** B **6.** C **7.** D **8.** B **9.** B **10.** A **11.** C **12.** A **13.** C
14. C

Alphabet Soup Puzzle 4 Solution

L	J	L	X	B	E	E	T	K
X	F	R	E	B	E	A	K	N
S	P	B	B	E	E	N	I	Z
B	E	E	C	H	L	F	X	G
M	B	A	S	S	C	P	I	O
J	V	K	M	B	A	S	E	Q
B	I	L	O	B	E	E	T	O
B	E	A	C	H	G	Z	F	U
W	X	B	E	A	T	Q	G	T
S	B	E	A	N	C	C	J	C

Word Maze Puzzle 5 Solution

P	Q	G	Y	J	T	I	Y	Z	R	R	R	T	H	B
V	R	J	P	J	A	H	M	V	I	B	E		B	E
N	W	V	M	Y	W	B	C	S	E	W	T	R	L	L
R	L	W	Q	C	J	N	D	M	L	B	H	R	C	W
I	T	B	N	E	P	F	C	N	C	U	A	E	D	D
B	U	L	L	L	W	H	W	G	Z	F	E	R	R	Y
B	H	F	W	W	V	U	T	L	L	E	B	Y	E	L
F	C	U	Y	T	H	V	A	E	B	B	O	W	B	E
P	H	T	M	A	O	C	R	A	E	U	L	B	Y	B
V	V	A	B	U	V	P	D	H	Z	G	R	G	R	U

Jumbled Letters Quiz 5 Answers

1. bow **2.** birth **3.** belle **4.** bury **5.** bell **6.** blew **7.** beau **8.** berth **9.** berry **10.** blue
11. bow

Word Shapes Puzzle 5 Solution

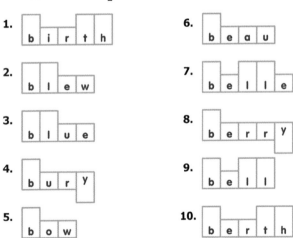

1. b i r t h
2. b l e w
3. b l u e
4. b u r y
5. b o w
6. b e a u
7. b e l l e
8. b e r r y
9. b e l l
10. b e r t h

Spelling Challenge Quiz 5 Answers

1. B **2.** C **3.** C **4.** A **5.** A **6.** D **7.** C **8.** B **9.** A **10.** C **11.** B

Alphabet Soup Puzzle 5 Solution

I	E	L	H	B	O	W	Z	D
E	R	D	M	B	U	R	Y	W
L	C	L	B	L	U	E	P	A
N	J	B	E	L	L	E	H	Y
C	M	V	Q	B	E	R	T	H
R	V	L	B	L	E	W	N	L
A	F	B	E	L	L	F	L	J
Z	B	O	B	I	R	T	H	F
K	B	E	R	R	Y	H	R	V
G	S	Z	T	B	E	A	U	N

Review Exercise 1 Answers

1. base **2.** heir **3.** berry **4.** bated **5.** ball **6.** bee **7.** aisle **8.** bow **9.** bade **10.** air **11.** bow **12.** berth **13.** bare **14.** birth **15.** beau **16.** bale **17.** beat **18.** belle **19.** bawl **20.** bass **21.** baron **22.** beet **23.** bass **24.** beach **25.** alter **26.** bawled **27.** isle **28.** bail **29.** bald **30.** all **31.** eight **32.** beat **33.** ate **34.** bear **35.** bean **36.** ale **37.** bury **38.** ball **39.** baron **40.** aloud **41.** baited **42.** be **43.** bear **44.** blue **45.** beat **46.** bail **47.** awl **48.** ant **49.** beech **50.** bad **51.** ail **52.** altar **53.** aunt **54.** allowed **55.** bell **56.** beer **57.** barren **58.** been **59.** blew

Review Exercise 2 Answers

1. bawled **2.** alter **3.** blew **4.** air **5.** bow **6.** belle **7.** beer **8.** all **9.** beet **10.** beat **11.** aunt **12.** awl **13.** barren **14.** bail **15.** allowed **16.** bee **17.** ball **18.** eight **19.** bated **20.** altar **21.** isle **22.** ate **23.** beat **24.** baited **25.** beau **26.** aloud **27.** be **28.** baron **29.** bald **30.** beech **31.** baron **32.** ail **33.** bass **34.** base **35.** berry **36.** ant **37.** bear **38.** bell **39.** birth **40.** berth **41.** ball **42.** been **43.** heir **44.** bear **45.** bale **46.** beach **47.** bawl **48.** bade **49.** base **50.** blue **51.** beat **52.** bean **53.** bass **54.** bow **55.** bare **56.** aisle **57.** bad **58.** bury **59.** ale **60.** bail

Test Yourself Answers

1. (ale)(ail) **2.** (heir)(air) **3.** (aisle)(Isle) **4.** (All)(awl) **5.** (allowed)(aloud) **6.** (alter)(altar)

7. (aunt)(ant) **8.** (ate)(eight) **9.** (bade)(bad) **10.** (Bail)(bale) **11.** (bated)(baited)

12. (bawled)(bald) **13.** (bawl)(ball) **14.** (baron)(barren) **15.** (beer)(bear)(bare)

16. (Be)(bee) **17.** (beech)(beach) **18.** (bass)(base) **19.** (bean)(been)

20. (beat) (beet)(beat) **21.** (beau)(bow) **22.** (belle)(bell) **23.** (bury)(berry)

24. (berth)(birth) **25.** (blew)(blue)

Volume 2 List 3 Spiral Puzzle Solution

B	U	Y	B	R	U	I
G	H	B	R	U	T	T
U	N	B	U	T	E	B
O	O	O	N	C	B	U
R	N	N	N	A	Y	T
O	A	C	E	Y	B	T
B	W	O	R	R	U	B

Volume 2 List 3 Matching Quiz Answers

1. canon **2.** but **3.** borough **4.** brute **5.** cannon **6.** bye **7.** bruit **8.** by **9.** butt
10. buy **11.** burrow

Volume 2 List 3 Crossword Puzzle Solution

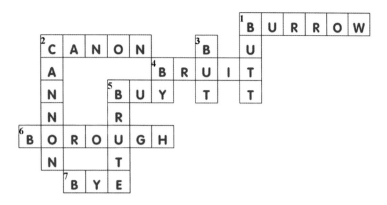

Volume 2 List 3 Spelling Challenge Quiz Answers

1. D. butt **2. A.** by **3. A.** brute **4. C.** bye **5. A.** buy **6. B.** borough **7. C.** bye **8. C.** canon **9. C.** burrow **10. C.** cannon **11. A** bruit **12. A.** but

Volume 2 List 3 Decoding Puzzle Solution

p	b	q	d	c	m	r	e	u	k	y	i	v
1	2	3	4	5	6	7	8	9	10	11	12	13
z	n	a	j	g	o	l	t	x	s	w	h	f
14	15	16	17	18	19	20	21	22	23	24	25	26

1. 2-11   by

2. 2-7-9-12-21   bruit

3. 2-11-8   bye

4. 5-16-15-15-19-15   cannon

5. 5-16-15-19-15   canon

6. 2-7-9-21-8   brute

7. 2-9-21   but

8. 2-9-7-7-19-24   burrow

9. 2-9-11   buy

10. 2-19-7-19-9-18-25   borough

11. 2-9-21-21   butt

ABOUT THIS BOOK

This book was commissioned by Dova Spelling City

www.dovaspellingcity.com

Spelling and Vocabulary for the 10 to 100 year old

24730986R00041

Printed in Great Britain
by Amazon